Zlatka Timenova   Alexandra Ivoylova

Cities of words
双 城 物 语

Lisbon   Sofia
里斯本   索菲亚

Sofia   Lisbon
索菲亚   里斯本

Златка Тименова   Александра Ивойлова

Градове от думи

Лисабон   София

София   Лисабон

Златка Тименова
Zlatka Timenova

Александра Ивойлова
Alexandra Ivoylova

Градове от думи

Cities of words

双 城 物 语

Лисабон
Lisbon
里斯本

София
Sofia
索菲亚

София
Sofia
索菲亚

Лисабон
Lisbon
里斯本

Lisboa oscilando como uma grande barca
Lisboa cruelmente construída ao longo da sua própria ausência
Digo o nome da cidade
– Digo para ver
Sophia de Mello Breyner Andresen (1977), in Obra Poética, 2011

Lisbon swaying like a sailing ship
Lisbon cruelly built during its own absence
I say the city's name
– I say it to see
Sophia de Mello Breyner Andresen (1977), in Obra Poética, 2011

Бълбукащи витрини,
вместо водопади.
Падащи неони,
вместо листа.
Цигари между пръстите,
вместо целувки,
вместо звезди.
Христина Мирчева, Потъване в сумрака, из Бялата сянка, 2017

Babbling shop windows,
instead of waterfalls.
Falling neons,
instead of leaves.
Cigarettes between the fingertips,
instead of kisses,
instead of stars.
Hristina Mircheva, Sinking into Dusk, From the collection White Shadow 2017

Preface

The book, titled "Cities of words: Lisbon – Sofia", written as a haiku dialogue between Zlatka Timenova and Alexandra Ivoylova, is about Lisbon and Sofia, the cities where we are living.

Our haiku are arranged following the seasons and are presented in three languages: Bulgarian (original) with translation in English and Chinese.

It is our second haiku dialogue book, the first one, titled "Traces of wind", is published in Sofia/Bulgaria in 2019.

Lisbon and Sofia are very old cities, full of history and modernity, natural beauty and cultural features. But, first of all, these are cities with a soul that create deep poetry emotions.

Our purpose is to present Lisbon and Sofia as they exist in our feelings, as objects of verbal art,…as cities of words. Living in a city, we hear the urban landscape speaking to our imagination, to our associations.

Writing haiku about urban space is a quite recent practice. But this is our everyday place, our imagination is spontaneously provoked by what we are seeing from the morning to the evening, from spring to winter. We registrate the changes of the wind, of the streets, the lights, the people, the gardens, the churches. We are alert to the changes of our feelings, of our eyes, of our appreciations. We invent the cities, thc cities invent us.

Our target audience will discover two of the oldest cities in Europe, presented as live beings, out of formal description and cold numbers. Our model of a reader could be the Baudelaire's "flâneur", or the modern traveller who is tired of concrete and glass and is looking for warm colours, human smiles and sadness.

In the present days is not very easy to travel physically. We propose to our reader a poetical journey, a trip in the imagination.
As the Portuguese poet Fernando Pessoa says:

„If I imagine, I see. What am I doing more, when I am travelling? Only the extreme weakness of the imagination legitimates the necessity to move around in order to feel. /Se imagino, vejo. Que mais faço eu se viajo? Só a fraqueza extrema da imaginação justifica que se tenha que deslocar para sentir. /"
Livro do Desassossego por Bernardo Soares, Vol. II, Fernando Pessoa/Lisboa: Atica, 1982.-387.

Zlatka Timenova

To Readers

Firstly, I'd like to express my sincere thanks to the poets for the enjoyment I derive from their poems, especially at such a moment when we are going through the epidemic. Their description of the four seasons with the flowers, the wind, the snow; the peddlers, tramps and lovers… brings me all the way to the far away countries, only to find daily life in the two cities takes on poetic air and colour.

For some time in history, Chinese people seem to have spent most of the time on poetry rather than science, and modern science was neglected while poetry got highly developed. As a result, there are many different poem structures and styles, with complexity or simplicity respectively.

As near neighbours, China and Japan influence each other a lot. Haiku is unique for its style. Its strict rules become optional as time goes on when Haiku get popular all over the world and are written in different languages.

As people know, it is challenging to get all the components in a poem into another language. Haiku, because of its extreme succinctness, becomes a good example.

The very limited lines and words leave large room for imagination. During my translation, I tried to convey ALL the components in each poem, missing as little as possible; and at the same time, to convey ONLY the existing components, applying as little as possible my own imagination or understanding. I put some extra words just for better effect and/or understanding when it was really necessary.

The culture of the two cities is essential for the translation. A lot of background knowledge of Lisbon and Sofia is required. I thankfully got a lot of help through my frequent discussion with the poets.

For some poems, I rearranged the lines, in order to make the meaning clearer and/or the sound more enjoyable. Occasionally, I made the lines rhyme. I followed the Japanese traditional 5-7-5 pattern when it was possible and seemed natural. Sometimes, I adopted the Chinese style, including the layout of the lines, the rhythm patterns.

I have to admit that at times, despite my efforts, I still cannot get eventually a satisfactory translation. Readers interested in Chinese language, you might try your own version to enrich the endless process of translation. I believe that you might enhance your pleasure and ease my mind.

Happy reading!

Liu, Wei
from Beijing

Онази странна тръпка…

That strange thrill…

怦 然 心 动…

Alexandra Ivoylova, Sofia

краят на февруари
зъзнат продавачите
на мартеници

the end of February
shivering peddlers
of Martenitzas[1]

春来二月终
贩夫瑟瑟行
马特内萨传真情

мартенско слънце
дълга целувка
при светофара

March sun
a lingering kiss
at the traffic-lights

三月的太阳
恋恋不舍热吻长
落在交通灯上

---

[1]Martenitza – a small piece of adornment made from red and white yarn which people traditionally exchange in March (all the notes concerning the poems about Sofia, are from the translator).

Zlatka Timenova, Lisbon

розмаринът
е особено напрегнат
но още е рано

the rosemary
is particularly tense
but it is still early

迷迭香
含苞欲放
为时尚早惹心慌

гълъбите са полудели
толкова гласовита
любов

the pigeons are crazy
such noisy
love

鸽子狂
恬噪响
为爱忙

Alexandra Ivoylova, Sofia

снежни върхове
зад нацъфтели клони
първи лястовици

snowy peaks
behind the sprouting branches
first swallows

枝杈新芽添
掩映雪山
飞燕初现

вечерен автобус
самотници
дишат в лицата си

an evening bus
loners breathing into
each other's faces

夜班公交车
陌路同行人
鼻息相与共

Zlatka Timenova, Lisbon

на площад "Росио"
дърветата цъфтят
очите ми стават сини

in Rossio Square
trees are in blossom
my eyes become blue

罗西奥广场
枝头繁花锦簇
映蓝我双眼

розов храст
в градината –
"Speak low when you speak, love"

rosebush
in the garden –
"Speak low when you speak, love"[2]

蔷薇丛中
爱语低声

"Speak low when you speak, love"

---

[2] A romantic song, composed by Kurt Weill, lyrics by Ogden Nash (all the notes concerning the poems about Lisbon, are from Zlatka Timenova).

Alexandra Ivoylova, Sofia

деца играят
със сапунени мехури
ефимерни вечности

children playing
with soap bubbles
ephemeral eternities

玩童
吹起肥皂泡
短暂的永恒

лилави сенки
над гроба на Поета
"люлека ми замириса"

blue dusk
over the poet's tomb
"the smell of lilac I recall"[3]

蓝色黄昏
诗人墓 坟
"丁香萦绕于心"

---

[3]"The smell of Lilac I recall" is a line taken from a popular poem by Ivan Vazov, one of the most revered Bulgarian poets.

Zlatka Timenova, Lisbon

странен блясък
в очите им
трамваят отминава

strange light
in their eyes
the tram is passing by

电车驶过
他们眼里
奇异光芒闪烁

"Алфама"
ограда в пламъци
бугенвилия

Alfama
a fence in flames
bougainvillea

在阿尔法玛区
篱笆如焰似火
紫亚兰花盛开

Alexandra Ivoylova, Sofia

слънчеви камбани
огласят утрото
Витоша още в сняг

sunny bells
chiming the morn
Vitosha[4] is still in snow

钟声朗朗
奏响黎明
维托莎仍在雪中

призрачни лица
по тъмните алеи
смартфони

ghostly faces
along dark allays
smartphones

面孔似幽灵
出没暗巷中
手机明复明

---

[4] Vitosha Mountain rises above the city of Sofia.

Zlatka Timenova, Lisbon

градът се плъзга
по водите на Тежу
днес и винаги

the city slides
on Tagus waters
today and always

乘着塔格斯河
城市滑行而过
古往今来无辍

сред тесните улици
луната се крие –
сплетени сенки

along the narrow streets
the moon is hiding –
interlaced shadows

街道狭窄
月亮藏躲 –
阴影交织

Alexandra Ivoylova, Sofia

индустриална зона
на билборда
изоставено гнездо

an industrial zone
above a billboard
a deserted nest

工业区
广告牌上
废弃的鸟巢

светкавици валят
пред фонтаните на театъра
вечерни срещи

lightening cascades
in front of the theatre fountains
evening dates

相约夜幕下
剧院喷泉前
流光溢彩炫

Zlatka Timenova, Lisbon

стара жена танцува
в топлата нощ –
изсъхнала роза

old lady dancing
in the hot night –
dry rose

夜来热不减
老妇舞翩翩
玫瑰花已干

смях и бира в нощта
корабът тръгва
след малко

fun and beer in the night
the ship sails away
in a while

夜阑人已静
欢愉啤酒中
须臾转瞬间
船将离岸行

Alexandra Ivoylova, Sofia

чезне
пъстротата на тревите
бръмчене на косачки

fading
hues of grasses
roar of lawnmowers

看绿草青青
转瞬间色去凋零
割草机轰鸣

гасне залезът
в стъклата на колите
задръстване

the sunset dwindles
in the windows of the cars
traffic-jam

车窗映落日
落日渐销蚀
交通阻塞迟

Zlatka Timenova, Lisbon

прозрачно облаче
само́ сред безкрайността
първият ден…

small transparent cloud
alone in infinity
the first day…

小小薄云一片
茫茫无限天穹
第一天…

реклама в метрото
очите на детето с цвят
на пролетни треви

advertising in the metro
eyes of a child have
the colour of spring grass

地铁的广告
孩子的双眸
颜色若春草

Alexandra Ivoylova, Sofia

цветни графити
изкачват обелиска
Братската могила

vibrant graffiti
climb up the obelisk
of the Brotherhood Mound[5]

醒目的涂鸦
高高画上了
盟兄纪念塔

тръгват си работниците
скелето на строежа
достига облака

the builders are leaving
the scaffolding reaches
the cloud

建筑工人将辞行
脚手架高耸
直逼云端触天顶

---

[5]The Mound of Brotherhood or Bratska Mogila is a monument in Sofia in commemoration of those who fought against fascism.

три стари фасади
разказват приказки –
градско изкуство

three old facades
are telling stories –
urban art

三个旧门面
讲述着古老的故事 -
城市艺术

в метрото
служители и туристи
еднакво отегчени

in the metro
employees and tourists
equally bored

在地铁里面
务工者抑或游客
同样的倦怠

И онази бавност…

And that slowness…

慵 懒 滞 缓…

Zlatka Timenova, Lisbon

по тротоарите
полепнали сенки
на дървета

on the pavement
the glued shadows
of trees

树木的阴影
粘粘的胶附在
人行道上

кафене край реката
минути разтеглени
до нищото

café by the river
minutes stretched away
into nothingness

河边咖啡馆中
时间得以延长
伸向空寂虚无

Alexandra Ivoylova, Sofia

най-дългият ден
цветовете на слънцето
по всички фасади

the longest day
colors of the sun
across the facades

最长的白昼
太阳的光彩
穿过了门廊

кафе „Монпарнас“
чаят ни стине
край купчина книги

café Montparnasse
our tea growing cold
next to a pile of books

蒙帕纳斯咖啡馆
在一堆书旁
茶已凉

трамвай nº28
се катери по хълма
времето тежи

tram nº28
climbing the hill
time is heavy[6]

28 路电车
负着岁月之重载
驶上了山坡

керамичните плочки
по фасадите
спират слънцето

the ceramic tiles
on the facades
block the sun

门面上的瓷砖
挡住了
骄阳

---

[6]Tram nº28 is an old emblematic tram in Lisbon.

Alexandra Ivoylova, Sofia

бавен залез
уличните лампи светват
преди звездите

a languid sunset
street lamps alight
before the stars

日落　懒洋洋
路灯已点亮
众星仍隐藏

"Summertime"
в чашата с джин
синя луна

"Summertime"
in the glass of gin
the blue moon

"Summertime"
回响在杜松子酒杯
月亮幽蓝

Zlatka Timenova, Lisbon

черно-бялата настилка
на тротоарите
издишва лятото

the black and white
pavement mosaics
exhale the summer

人行道
马赛克黑白相间
呼出夏日的气息

изведнъж на "Шиадо"
италиански канцонети
отнасят следобеда

suddenly in Chiado
Italian songs blow away
the afternoon

在基亚多
意大利歌曲
瞬间吹散了
午后时光

Alexandra Ivoylova, Sofia

пълнолуние
щурците ли нажежават
мрака?

full moon
is it the crickets firing
the darkness?

满月
暗夜中
蟋蟀在点火？

нощни булеварди
блусът на града
отеква в мен

midnight boulevards
the blues of the city
resounds within me

午夜的大道
城市布鲁斯
在心中回荡

Zlatka Timenova, Lisbon

августовски нощи
чайки и хора спят
на плажа в Кашкаиш

August nights
seagulls and people sleep
on the Cascais beach

八月的夜晚
海鸥和人们睡在
喀什基海滩

пред църквата
птичи хор посреща
процесията

in front of the church
a choir of birds
meets the procession

教堂前
鸟雀唱诗班
迎候信徒的队列

Alexandra Ivoylova, Sofia

далечна мълния
градът обърнат
в локвите

distant lightening
the city inverted
in puddles

远处闪电
城市倒映
积水片片

излизаме
от хайку изложба
вея си с японско ветрило

coming out
of a haiku exhibition
I flutter a Japanese fan

步出
俳句展
摇动日本扇

Zlatka Timenova, Lisbon

улиците на Лисабон
говорят на всички езици
юлски ден

the streets of Lisbon
speak all languages
July day

七月天
里斯本街头
说着各色语言

свечеряване
лек бриз събужда
града

twilight
a soft breeze
awakens the city

暮光
和风
拂醒睡城

Alexandra Ivoylova, Sofia

Mall of Sofia
гигантски реклами пулсират
по сградите отсреща

Mall of Sofia
huge neon ads pulsate
on the buildings opposite

索非亚商区
巨大的广告霓虹
在对面的建筑上跃动

плисна дъжд
смях и викове
под старите кестени

spattering rain
laughter and screams
under the old chestnut trees

雨水飞溅
老栗树下
笑叫人欢

Zlatka Timenova, Lisbon

гореща нощ
площадите танцуват
бразилски ритми

hot night
the squares dance
in Brazilian rhythms

夜来热透
舞蹈随着
巴西节奏

кино в парка
на първия ред
жена и куче

cinema in the park
first row
a lady and a dog

公园影院
在第一排
女人和狗

Alexandra Ivoylova, Sofia

любовен смях
сладоледът
капе по ръкава ми

love laughter
ice cream
trickles down my sleeve

笑语含爱声朗朗
随着冰淇淋
滴落在我袖子上

витрини
сред отразените тълпи
изящни манекени

shop windows
among reflected crowds
exquisite mannequins

商店橱窗里
优雅的服装模特儿
跻身熙来攘往的人群映像

Zlatka Timenova, Lisbon

разходка в нощта
нов град изплува
в тишината

walking in the night
new city emerges
from the silence

夜来漫步行
物静人无声
旧城展新貌
万籁俱寂中

Alexandra Ivoylova, Sofia

удължени сенки
войни от бронз
в окото на залеза

elongated shadows
warriors of bronze
in the eye of sunset

拉长的影子
在落日眼中
乃青铜武士

Есен, винаги…

Autumn, always…

秋 来 秋 去…

Alexandra Ivoylova, Sofia

пейка в Южния парк
любовни думи
забравени

a bench in South Park[7]
love words
forgotten

卿卿我我的情话
被遗忘在
南方公园长凳上

пламнали прозорци
изпращат деня
вечерен вятър

incandescent windows
sending the day away
evening breeze

窗棂炎炎
白昼依依
迎晚风习习

---

[7] South Park is one of the largest parks in Sofia.

езеро в парка
лебед размесва
облаци и листа

lake in the park
a swan mixing
clouds with leaves

园中湖面上
天鹅搅混
落叶与浮云

луната се търкаля
по покривите
на Лисабон

the moon is rolling
on the roofs
of Lisbon

圆月
在里斯本屋顶上
滚动

Alexandra Ivoylova, Sofia

Орлов мост
над арките му
никой не спира

Eagles Bridge
above its arches
no one stops

鹰桥
桥拱上
无人驻足

площад „Независимост“
старият инвалид продава
знамена

Independence Square
the old cripple peddles
flags

独立广场上
跛行老贩夫
旗帜一面面

Zlatka Timenova, Lisbon

тераса над „Лапа“
реката и небето
се сливат

terrace in Lapa
the river and the sky
in fusion

拉帕露台
见
河天一色

бездомникът сгъва
грижливо одеялото си
пред театъра

homeless man doubling
his blanket carefully
by the Theatre

剧院旁
流浪汉
认真折起睡毯

Alexandra Ivoylova, Sofia

вятър пилее листата
прибрани от метачите
неделя

the wind scatters the leaves
piled up by the sweepers
Sunday

清扫工聚起落叶
风起又吹散
星期日

дворът на училището
сюрия деца ме викат
в друго време

the school yard
a flock of children is calling me
from another time

校园里
一群孩子在叫我
恍若隔世

Zlatka Timenova, Lisbon

тих дъжд
мислите ми
се отдръпват

silent rain
my thoughts
are vanishing

雨落无声
万千思绪
无影无踪

един глас връща
времето назад –
фадо

a voice turns
time back –
fado

声声入耳
曲曲思乡
时光倒流

Alexandra Ivoylova, Sofia

кафене на гарата
на дъното на чашите
горчива утайка

a café at the station
at the bottom of the cups
bitter grounds

车站咖啡厅
杯底
苦的沉淀

есенни улици
по стъклата на автобуса
следи от летен дъжд

autumn streets
on bus windows
the remains of summer rain

街巷已入秋
公交车窗上
夏日雨痕留

Zlatka Timenova, Lisbon

ако не съм благодарила
попитай брезата
в нашия парк

if I haven't thanked
ask the birch
in our parc

我是否未表谢忱
到我们园中
去向那白桦发问

едно листо пада
погледът ми проследява
тишината

a leaf is falling
my eyes follow
the silence

一片叶子下落
我二目相随
一片沉默

Alexandra Ivoylova, Sofia

прегръдка
сред окапалите листи
сбогом на цветовете

an embrace
among the fallen leaves
farewell to colors

落叶
相拥
告别色彩

ветровито
разпилени край контейнера
черно-бели снимки

windy
scattered by the garbage bin
black and white photos

风起
黑白照片
吹散在垃圾桶边

върху зелената трева
сухи клонки
пролетно-есенно ми е

on the green grass
dry thin branches
spring-autumn feeling

绿草地上
枯枝纤细
恍若春秋

есенни празници
на френското кино
Лисабон е Париж

autumn fest
of the French cinema
Lisbon is Paris

秋季的
法国电影节
里斯本变成巴黎

Alexandra Ivoylova, Sofia

небето гасне
надраскано от самолети
ято врани

the sky is fading
scratched by planes
a flock of crows

天色渐暗
飞机划过
一群乌鸦

площад „Славейков"
търся духа
на поетите

Slaveykov Square
I'm searching for the spirit
of the poets

斯拉夫科夫广场
我在寻找
诗人的灵魂

Zlatka Timenova, Lisbon

свечеряване
гълъбите чистят деня
от крилете си

twilight
the pigeons clean the day
from their wings

夜幕降临
鸽子用翅膀
清理一日光阴

залез над реката
по-бавен
от бавните води

sunset over the river
slower
than the slow waters

河上日落
缓缓
比水流更慢

Alexandra Ivoylova, Sofia

нови графити
по избелелите врати
война на думи

fresh graffiti
on bleak doors
a war of words

门扉幽暗
新画的涂鸦
唇枪舌战

Zlatka Timenova, Lisbon

слънчево утро
колко време трябва
за да си отиде лятото

sunny morning
how long does the summer take
to leave

清晨就晴空日朗
还要等多久
夏天才姗姗离去

Зимен ден, помисли си тя

Winter day, she thought

冬日，她暗自思忖

Alexandra Yvoylova, Sofia

първи сняг
замръзва на двора
последната роза

first snow
freezing in the yard
is the last rose

冰封的庭院里
初雪
像最后一朵玫瑰

сняг вали
над руините на Сердика
сенките растат

it is snowing
over the ruins of Serdika
the shadows are growing

下雪了
塞尔迪卡废墟
阴影越拉越长

Zlatka Timenova, Lisbon

килим от жълти листа
зимата е дошла тихо
тази нощ

carpet of yellow leaves
winter had come silently
this night

一夜间
黄叶铺地看似毯
悄然而至是冬天

дъждовни капки
осветени от луната –
снежинки…

rain drops
in the moonlight –
snowflakes…

月光下
雨滴 -
雪花…

Aleksandra Ivoylova, Sofia

светли домове елхи
шейнички - търся картичка
за Лисабон

looming houses Christmas trees
and sleighs - looking for a postcard
for Lisbon

房舍　圣诞树　雪橇
若隐若现–在找寻
寄往里斯本的明信片

между две грейнали елхи
механичните движения
на Дядо Коледа

between two shining Christmas trees
the mechanical movements
of Santa Claus

闪亮的圣诞树间
是圣诞老人
在机械的运动着

Zlatka Timenova, Lisboa

в Лисабон
само Коледната елха
е покрита със сняг

in Lisbon
only the Christmas tree
is covered with snow

在里斯本
唯圣诞树
被雪覆盖

снежен човек
от пластмасови чашки
къде е носът му?

snowman
of plastic caps
where is his nose?

雪人
塑料帽子
不见了鼻子？

Alexandra Ivoylova, Sofia

зачервени ръце
продавачка на топли гевреци
в студа

red hands
a woman selling warm bagels
in the cold

双手红通通
伫立寒风中
妇人卖热饼

отминава свети Валентин
цветарката в магазина
сама

Valentine's Day is over
the flower woman in the shop
alone

圣瓦伦廷节已过
茕茕孑立卖花女
形影相吊守店中

Zlatka Timenova, Lisbon

стара жена храни
бездомните котки –
не трепери от студ

an old woman feeds
the alley cats –
she doesn't shiver

老妪态龙钟
巷中把猫喂 –
不再颤巍巍

краят на февруари
туристите се връщат
от плаж

end of February
the tourists return
from the beach

二月底
从海滨
游客们回来了

Alexandra Ivoylova, Sofia

празнична глъчка
жълтее в снега
изпуснат лимон

festive clamour
in the snow the yellow
of a fallen lemon

节日的喧嚣
雪中的桔黄
落下的柠檬

по прозорците
премигват светлинки
морзът на нощта

windows
with blinking little lights
the Morse Code of the night

窗户扇扇
时明时暗
莫尔斯电码在夜间

следобедът
и котката ми
еднакво сиви

the afternoon
and my cat
equally grey

下午
如同我的猫
一样的灰色

улица „Аугуща“
зимните палта са
само на витрините

Augusta Street
the winter coats are
only in shop windows

奥古斯塔街上
冬衣只出现在
店铺的橱窗

Alexandra Ivoylova, Sofia

снежни алеи
черни дървета
шепотът на изпращачите

snowy allays
black trees
whispers of goodbye

雪巷
黑树
道别声轻

здрачава се
от всяко дихание
литва облаче

nightfall
from every breath
a cloud flies up

夜幕降临
随着呼吸
雾升云起

Zlatka Timenova, Lisbon

буря в морето
чайка срещу вятъра
Джонатан…?

storm at sea
a seagull against the wind
Jonathan...?[8]

海上风暴生
海鸥逆势行
乔纳森…?

мост над Тежу
Новогодишна заря
оцветява мъглата

bridge over the Tagus
the New Year fireworks
colour the mist

塔格斯桥上空
新年的焰火
给薄雾染上颜色

---

[8]Richard Bach, Jonathan Livingston Seagull, ed. Macmillan Inc,1970.

Alexandra Ivoylova, Sofia

взривове от фойерверки
старата и новата година
си поделят нощта

explosions of fireworks
the Old and New Years
are sharing the night

炸响是烟花
旧岁与新年
共度此良宵

Коледна вечер
клошарят вади бутилка
пред луксозен хотел

Christmas Eve
the tramp takes out a bottle
outside a luxury hotel

平安夜
豪华酒店外
流浪汉掏出酒瓶

Zlatka Timenova, Lisbon

Свята нощ
бездомникът
ми се усмихва

Holy night
the homeless man
smiles at me

圣善平安夜
无家可归者
报我以微笑

вълните гонят чайките
към брега
някои няма да стигнат…

the waves are chasing
the seagulls to the shore
some will not arrive…

浪逐海鸥
冲向岸边
或有不逮…

Alexandra Ivoylova, Sofia

вали, вали …
все по-далече в снега
кварталът на детството

it's snowing, snowing...
so far away in the whiteness
the street of my childhood

雪，下雪了…
苍茫遥远的白色
带我回到童年的街巷

Zlatka Timenova, Lisbon

облаци отнасят
зимното слънце
плач на бебе

clouds carry away
the winter sun
a baby cries

云飞云舞
挟冬日而去
孩童啼哭

Postface

Писахме тези хайку, когато светът все още пътуваше свободно, когато разстоянията бяха преодолени и животът в градовете кипеше във вихъра на многоцветните сезони. Днес прегради затварят пътищата на човека и той се отправя към себе си, в безкрая на духовните пространства. Така и нашият стремеж да пътуваме чрез създадените от нас „градове от думи" придоби нов смисъл. Хайку – тази най- лаконична поезия, ни дава свободата да откриваме други пътища – онези ефирни и ненакърними нишки, които ни свързват. Нашите градове тук все още пулсират в ритъма на многолюдния полис, на градския шум или моментното усамотение, на оживлението и празниците, на светлината и мрака... Шепата слова разкриват своите полета на премълчаното. За да поканим читателя да пренесе в тях собствените си преживявания.

Така както белият цвят съдържа целия спектър от цветове, така тишината носи звучностите на света. Пред нас е белотата на листа и тишината между думите в хайку. Тишината – *«неограничена, безкрайна и по-богата от човешката мъдрост»* (Бан'я Нацуиши).

Александра Ивойлова

We wrote these Haiku poems when people were still free to travel, when distances were being overcome and the hustling and bustling cities were in the colorful whirl of the seasons. Today, barriers block the highways and man has set on a journey through the spiritual infinity of the inner-self. Therefore, our desire to travel through the 'cities of words' that we create, has taken on a new meaning. Haiku, this most succinct form of poetry, gives us the means to discover other roads, which are the airy and resilient threads that connect us. Our cities still pulsate with the rhythm of the multitudinous polis – with noises and moments of solitude, with flurry of feasts, and with light and darkness... The handful of words uncovers fields of the unsaid where we invite the reader to transport his own experience.

Like the colour white, which bears the whole spectrum of colours, silence bears the whole sonority of the world. Before us we have the whiteness of the page and the silence between the words in the Haiku. The silence – *"limitless, infinite and rich beyond human wisdom"* (Ban'ya Natsuishi).

Alexandra Ivoylova

NOTA
PLATE

ZLATKA TIMENOVA-VALTCHEVA obtained Academic Degree Docteur-ès- Lettres, University of Sofia, Bulgária, and Doctor of Modern Languages and Literatures, University of Coimbra, Portugal, subject: "Le silence littéraire et ses formes dans l'œuvre romanesque de Marguerite Duras". She is publishing articles and books chapters about literary critics, French literature, theory of translation, comparative literature, poetry.

She is a member of: CLEPUL of Universidade de Lisboa; ICLA; COMPARES; WHA; PEN-club Bulgaria; FHA (French haiku association); EUROPOESIE, France.

Published Poetry in journals and antologies: Bulgarian journal *Plamak*, n° 3/4, 2009 ; n° 1/2, 2010, Sofia; Portuguese journals *Babilónia*, n° 4, 2006; n° 10/11, 2011, Lisboa; *DiVersos*, n° 23, Lisboa, 2015; English journal: *Blithe Spirit*, vol.26, n° 3, 2016; Japanese journal: *Ginyu*, n° 77, 2018. *Des herbes enlacées*, haiku in Bulgarian, French, Japanese ; French journal: *GONG*, n° 62, 2019; Cyberwit's International journal, *TAJ MAHAL*, vol.16, number1, June 2017; *Sonos e Sonhos*, Chiado Ed., Lisbon, 2014, 2016; *WHA Anthology*, Tokyo, 2015, 2016, 2017, 2018, 2019; *World haiku*, 2016, Morocco; *World haiku conference anthology*, Parma, 2017, Anthology of Haiku-club Viet-Nâm, 2019.

Published Poetry online: http://literatensviat.com, n° 24, 2010, and n° 33, 2011 ; *Living haiku anthology*, Under the Bashô, 2016;.*Sharpening the green pencil*, 2016;.2nd Symposium Haiku Viet Nâm, 2016.

Books:

Chama, a palavra, (in Portuguese and French), Edlp Editora, Lisboa, 2013.

Comme un oiseau contre le vent, Ed. Encres Vives, coll. Ancres blanches, Colomiers, France, 2013.

As a Star dust (in Bulgarian), Ed. Plamak, Sofia, 2013.

Escrito no vento (in French and Portuguese), with Casimiro de Brito. Ed. Eufeme, Leça de Palmeira, 2017.

Fim de tarde (in Bulgarian, Portuguese, English, Japanese), Ed. Eufeme, Leça de Palmeira, 2018.

Traces of wind (in Bulgarian, Portuguese, English), haiku dialogue with Alexandra Ivoylova, ed. Karina M, 2019.

L'ombre d'un arbre sur un mur (in Bulgarian, French, Arabic). Ed. Kénitra, Morocco,2019.

Publications about haiku: *Le haiku, couleur de femme*. In: World haiku, 2016, n°12, Shichigatsudo, Tokyo.; *L'élan du haiku slave*. In: Arabic haiku and world haiku poetics, Second haiku seminar, Oujda, Morocco, 2016; *L'(im)possible beauté du paysage urbain dans le haïku*. In: World Haïku, 2018, n° 14, Shichigatsudo, Tokyo; *Haiku and self-translation*, Seminar in CNRS, Paris, 2019 (invited speaker).

ALEXANDRA IVOYLOVA is graduated as a pianist from the National Academy of Music "Prof. Pancho Vladigerov" in Sofia. She has specialized with the well-known concert pianist and pedagogue Eric Heidsieck in Paris and studied chamber-singing. As a mezzo-soprano she has issued the compact disk "Baroque arias and songs", presenting works of Handel, Purcell, Caccini, Caldara, Scarlatti, Pergolesi and some others. Her second compact disc "Reflections – poetry and music" was created by the Bulgarian composer N. Dobrinov after her book in Bulgarian and French.

Alexandra Ivoylova takes part in artistic exhibitions, illustrates literature pages in the press. As an author, she has shown 70 etchings in an organ concert slide-show (the first in Bulgaria; organist S. Levy). Her one-man show of photo haiga "Shadows & Lights" was opened in the American corner in Sofia, 28th Days of Japanese Culture, 2017. Al. Ivoylova publishes essays, fragments, poetry (including poetry for children), literature, art and musical critiques.

She has issued the books "Bitter rains", "Hommages", and "A way above the world" (in Bulgarian) – poems; "Reflections" (in Bulgarian and French) – haiku; "Unexpected thoughts" (in Bulgarian) – maxims; "Resonances" (in Bulgarian, co-author S. Filipova) – poetic dialogues; "The last rose" (in Bulgarian) – haibun; "Alongside stanzas" (in Bulgarian and English, co-author Al. Dabnishki, images J. Stankova) – poetic dialogues; "Traces of wind" (in Bulgarian, French and English, co-author Z. Timenova) – haiku; "The entity of Botev's speech" (in Bulgarian) – analyses. She is the compiler and editor of the Bulgarian-French bilingual haiku anthology "The town" – 103 Bulgarian, French and Francophone poets.

Her haiku are published in nine languages in paper support and online, as well as in the anthologies such as WHA-Anthology (since 2005), Constanta 2013, Capoliveri 2015, Haikouest 2015, the Anthology of Haiku-club Viet-Nâm, 2019, etc.

Al. Ivoylova is a member of Bulgarian PEN-Center, World Haiku Association (WHA Japan), Union of Bulgarian Journalists, Bulgarian Haiku Union, Rencontres Européennes Europoésie, France.

She is a member of the editorial staff of the Bulgarian magazine "Haiku World".

The creative achievements of Al. Ivoylova include literary-musical readings – author's poetry and musical performances.

Alexandra Ivoylova

Zlatka Timenova